GATHERING THE CHURCH IN THE SPIRIT

Reflections on Exile and the Inscrutable Wind of God

WALTER BRUEGGEMANN

cts
PRESS

Adapted from the speech, "New Issues and Challenges for the Faithful" made by Walter Brueggemann at Nanjing Theological Seminary in Nanjing, China on June 3, 1994.

Design by Melissa Mahoney

ISBN 1-885121-16-4

CTS Press
P.O. Box 520
Decatur, GA 30031

I.
The Church Faces New Challenges

Because I am an Old Testament teacher and researcher, neither a theologian nor a cultural critic, it is necessary for me to approach my topic from the perspective of Old Testament texts. At the same time fully recognize that such an approach may strike one as remote from the challenges to the contemporary church.

Nonetheless, when I bring the issue of "The Churches in a Changing Society" to the Old Testament, I find contemporary crises readily connected to Old Testament issues. We may identify two major "church/society" changes in ancient Israel. One concerns the transition from tribal to royal society, the emergence of centralized political and economic power with its inevitable concomitant, centralization of worship and knowledge. This is a much studied transition in ancient Israel and may perhaps have modest parallels in the United States to the Industrial Revolution in the last century, and in China to the Revolution of 1948.[1] The other major transition of society in the Old Testament is the move from monarchal society into exile, with the collapse of the domination by a royal-temple apparatus, and Jewish marginalization into increasingly universalizing empires, Persian, Greek, and Roman.[2]

I shall argue, for the purpose of this discussion,

that that profound disestablishment which pervades everything about Israel's ancient faith is in important ways paralleled in the United States, by the emergence of something popularly called post-industrial, post-Enlightenment, or post-modern society. All of this language is used to refer to the deep cultural changes taking place in the Western world whereby old patterns of knowledge and power are no longer secure.

Thus I suggest that the current crisis of the U.S. Church closely parallels the ancient experience of Jews going into exile.[3] I begin with a probe about what happened to that community of faith, its faith and its praxis, in a context of such radical and comprehensive displacement. The repositioning (or depositioning) of Israel and its faith required enormously bold actions and strategies in order to be at all faithful or viable, or perhaps even to survive. In posing the issue in this way and in suggesting this parallel, I intend to suggest that the U.S. Church as we know it is now increasingly depositioned. That is, the church as an institutional force is being pushed out of the center of public life, no longer commanding great respect or exercising great social influence. In such a context, the church, in my judgment, must undertake bold actions and strategies in order to be at all faithful or viable or perhaps even to survive.

The new situation in which believing Israel found itself in the sixth century BCE is popularly termed "exile." In articles in *Theology Today* and *Journal for Preachers*, I have attempted to show how the experience, memory, and metaphor of exile

Gathering the Church in the Spirit

may be helpful for us, both in understanding our society and its current deep changes, and in discerning how and in what ways the church may face its missional existence in a context of displacement.[4]

I have suggested that the metaphor of "exile" may be understood among persons in the United States in two distinct ways. First, in a broadly cultural way the "homeland" in which all of us in the United States have grown up has been defined and dominated by white, male, Western assumptions. "Exile comes as those values and modes of authority are being effectively and progressively diminished."[5] With that dismissal, we are now required to live in a new situation that for many of us seems less like home. In such a context, folk need pastoral, theological help in relinquishing a "home" that is gone, and entry into a new, dangerous place that we sense as deeply "other."

Second, I have suggested an ecclesiological (church) exile in the same context. "Serious, reflective Christians find themselves increasingly at odds with the dominant values of consumer capitalism and its supportive military patriotism; there is no easy or obvious way to hold together core faith claims and the social realities around us."[6]

On both counts, civil and ecclesiological, I have suggested a) "loss of a structured, reliable 'world' where b) treasured symbols of meaning are mocked and dismissed."[7] Now I think one need not agree with all the nuances I give the matter or the judgments I have made, in order to agree that something of this massive change is taking place in our culture, and in the West generally.[8] Nor do I suggest that these changes are unmitigatedly bad, though many who are comfortable and privileged in old arrangements view the changes in a completely negative way. Whatever else, the changes are deep and enormous, probably irreversible, and require attention. Moreover, they require and permit the church to face its context in quite different, intentional ways.

Christopher Seitz, a young scholar at Yale, has shown that the situation of exile in ancient Israel created profound disputes among Jews over a correct reading of historical experience, and over reshaping communal power and authority.[9] He evidences the book of Jeremiah as a showcase for such disputed claims, especially between Jews in Babylon and Jews in the homeland.[10] That situation of conflictual interpretation lasted at least until the time of Ezra, when a new hegemony was established around Torah-Judaism which gave dominant shape to enduring Judaism, and identified the leaders who would conduct the normative interpretations for Judaism. The exile itself was a situation in which there was no such prevailing authority, but only competitors, each of which had to make its best case.

Our own situation, a situation of problematic pluralism is, I suggest, an approximate parallelism, in which a variety of interpretive voices compete in order to establish their version (or sub-version) of reality as correct.[11] By "pluralism" we mean a situation in which there are many competing voices without an agreed consensus as a starting place. It may well be that we shall arrive at a new consensus reading of faith and experience. We shall not arrive at

Gathering the Church in the Spirit ✦

such a consensus, however, until some "Ezra" arises in the right circumstances and is able to override all competitors and have a "final" say. In any case, we shall not return to any pre-exilic consensus as the Jews did not, even though there is a profound yearning for such a return.[12]

The evidence we have from that ancient displacement is that exile produced rich and varied theological literature which provides the main substance of the Hebrew canon, which is essentially a product of the exile.[13] It is as though the exile broke all established theological-political-interpretive restraints and all sorts of voices rushed to produce literature, some of it especially eloquent and daring, some of it requiring the production or invention of a new genre for proper and full articulation. It is as though new voices sounded which never before had been necessary and which, we may believe, had never before been permitted.

a) The Deuteronomist, the theology that grew out of the book of Deuteronomy, re-visioned the whole of Israel's remembered past in terms of the Torah and issues of obedience and disobedience.[14] This peculiarly dominant theological tradition wanted to give little credit to power politics and insisted that all of history, even exile, manifests a resilient moral shape. Consequently much of the literature after Deuteronomy either agreed and supported that claim (as in the Chronicler) or protested against it (Lamentations, Job). In any case, Israel could not ever again be done with a Deuteronomic shaping of reality, not ever.

b) The Priestly tradition includes biblical texts

that reflect the concerns of priests. These texts, usually dated to the period of the exile, represent the primary competition to the Deuteronomic tradition — paying little attention to "Torah obedience" as sponsored by the Deuteronomist but reflecting primarily upon the crisis of God's presence (and absence) in a seemingly abandoned world.[15] It was in the exile that the glory had indeed departed from Israel. In an extraordinary act of imagination, this tradition pressed Israel's faith to the large vista of creation, and then attended to particular priestly rules and procedures, suggesting decisive parallels between the right ordering of worship and the right ordering of creation, right ordering being both the pre-condition and the mode of God's presence.[16]

c) The completed book of Job, likely dated to this same exilic period, takes up old speech patterns of ancient Israel in order to construct a profound argument about the character of God, the reliability of God, and the fairness of God. The writer entertains the thought that God's moral order is unreliable, and that human courage is required to move beyond old absolutist claims.[17] The crisis about God in Job is called "theodicy," the wonderment about whether God is Just.

d) Finally I mention the great prophetic efforts of the exile, Jeremiah, Ezekiel, and II Isaiah.[18] These poetic, imaginative figures looked the discontinuity of experience in the face, and then dared to posit an unextrapolated newness...new covenant, new shepherd, new homecoming... wrought by the very God who moved beyond obedience, presence, or theodicy into new dimensions of faithfulness.

Gathering the Church in the Spirit ⚲

This remarkable effort in "moving beyond" settled consensus and orthodoxy issues in what I think are two pertinent observations. First, this creative activity provided the material for canonization which is commonly associated with Ezra. When it was finally agreed upon which books were to be included in scripture, the argument resulted in a remarkable, accommodating settlement. No single party or position was permitted total domination. Rather the biblical canon represented a compromise arrangement in which parties to the disputes evoked by displacement were given voice. Through these several positions, which came to be canonical, subsequent interpreters are permitted their trajectory of discernment which came to be regarded as revelatory. That is, pluralism lives at the very core of the Judaism, even in the Bible, worked out in the shadow of the exile.[19]

Second, while the formation of the biblical canon is a theological-literary activity, we should not miss the political gains and losses that are at stake in the process of canonization. Every interpretive position carries with it the authority, prestige, and privilege of its interpreters, so that pluralism is never only an interpretive, theological matter, but always a covert or overt political struggle.[20] The Old Testament, as it emerged out of exile, reflects a) the strenuous character of that political struggle and, b) the wisdom of the Jews, both to permit no one to dominate and to allow none to disappear completely. The pluralism of displacement perhaps requires a kind of civility that listens as well as speaks.

Finally, in my preliminary comments, I want to

focus on an article by Sigmund Mowinckel published in the *Journal of Biblical Literature* in 1934.[21] Mowinckel, a distinguished Norwegian scholar, observed a remarkable distinction between the early "ecstatic" prophets (including Elijah and Elisha) and the Reform Prophets, the ones we usually mean by the term "prophetic" (Isaiah, Amos, Jeremiah). Mowinckel observed that the early prophets rely upon the "spirit of Yahweh," but in the Reform prophets such as Isaiah and Jeremiah, the "spirit of Yahweh" plays almost no role, for these prophets are bearers of the "word of Yahweh." Mowinckel only hints, and I wish to emphasize, that with the coming of the exile, at the end of the period of the reforming prophets, the spirit reappears in the rhetoric of Isaiah 48-55 (in limited ways) , and much more in Ezekiel and Isaiah 56-66. Thus I do not dwell upon Mowinckel's primary point, but take a cue from him and move into the exilic period, while still attending to his categories of notice. The point suggested to me is that *in highly organized, institutionalized Yahwism of the monarchal period, the spirit had no room in which to operate. In the exilic period, however, with the termination of institutional support and restraint, Israel's life becomes again an arena for the reemergence of the "spirit of Yahweh" as a driving, compelling, liberating force.*

My suggestion then is quite specific. It is this: churches in the United States which now face the loss of their old centrality and influence and authority must attend to the new leadings of the spirit of God. The spirit of God is of course our teacher and comforter, so that we may expect to be taught, led, and cared for. But the spirit of God is also a free, unfettered "force" in the world, sent to blow away all that is old and failed, sent to blow newness among us that is unexpected and unplanned. All through the life and history of the church, God's spirit has come into the world to keep the people of God unsettled, open, on the move, and in obedient mission in fresh ways. Such spirit-focused faith can be a terrible threat to what is old and settled in the church. But it can also be a wondrous new opportunity for the church to be truly the church in mission.

II.
Texts of "Spirit"

I now propose to consider a series of texts that are conventionally dated in or just after the exile. My purpose is to consider specifically how this "changing society" of the ancient Jews was the place where God's spirit came, and the ways in which the community of faith in this context found itself unexpectedly moved by the spirit and in this time of emergency, was responsive to the spirit. I will mention seven texts, most of which are familiar to you.

1. *Isaiah 42:1-4.* The so-called "suffering servant" is notoriously enigmatic, so that I will proceed cautiously in relation to that vexed question. Nonetheless, in Isaiah 42:1, the conventional first mention of the servant who is chosen and upheld by Yahweh, the servant has a crucial mission, for which the coastlands wait. Three times in these verses, it is the work of this unidentified servant, presumably Israel, to bring justice in its most sweeping scope:

> He will bring *justice* to the nations . .
> he will faithfully bring forth *justice* . .
> he will not fail or be discouraged,
> till he has established *justice* in the earth.

In the context of Isaiah 48-55, commonly dated to the exile, "justice among the nations" apparently means an act which liberates all the exiled Jews, an act of power that confounds the "host" empires and gives to the outcast Jews freedom and impetus to return home to their own life.

Such a task, in any realistic thinking, is impossible, because the host empires did not want to lose their Jews, a form of cheap labor. Thus the liberation and enactment of justice must be an act of uncommon authority and force. And no "servant" could initiate such a daring possibility. Except, the very first verse authorizing the servant, has God say,

I have put my spirit upon him.

The spirit is an outrageous empowerment that permits actions which are completely disproportionate to capacity. The spirit undoes all conventional notions about what is possible, and addresses itself in the very historical process to what the world regards as impossible. Moreover, the poem ends in 42:9 with the assertion, "New things I now declare." In context this newness is the end of exile and the restoration of the historical process of Israel, which the great empires are helpless to resist. II Isaiah's rhetoric is saturated with creation language, so that we may suggest that the wind that blows new Israel is the same wind that blew an ordered creation out of chaos (Gen. 1:2).[22] This poetry focuses on something inscrutable and inexplicable, large and soon to be visible, for the world is not without this impulse to form that comes in God's inscrutable way. In our own time we are watching specific human agents enact God's will for justice. Such agents may include Nelson Mandela of South Africa, Jimmy

Carter, and many lesser people who operate in local ways.

2. *Isaiah 52:14-53:2.* I mention this familiar and enigmatic text only in passing. It does not have within it the term "spirit," and may not be useful to our reflection. But a thought occurred to me about 52:14 and 53:2:

> His appearance was so marred
>   beyond human resemblance,
> and his form beyond that of the sons of men...

> He had no form or comeliness
>   that we should look at him,
> and no beauty that one should desire him.

The term "form" in both uses is *ta'ar*, (which means a pleasing physical appearance). The text describes the servant as one who is physically repulsive. It is this very one, however, who will prosper and be satisfied, and be righteous and have offspring.

The emphasis upon form and appearance perhaps may be subsumed under II Isaiah's creation theology which is chronologically and thematically related to Genesis 1. ("Second Isaiah" refers to Isaiah 48-55, a part of the book of Isaiah dated a long time after Isaiah 1-39.) The creation, powered and shaped by God's "spirit," ends with the verdict "very good," i.e., "very lovely," made so by the spirit (Gen. 1:31).[23] Could it be that even this uncreated, unformed, unattractive servant becomes a subject of well-being, created as "very good, very lovely" by the same God who so forms the world by spirit in Gen. 1:2? Sometimes ordinary people who attract no great attention turn out to be agents of healing and transformation.

3. *Ezekiel 37:1-14.* When we come to Ezekiel, we are into a rhetorical enterprise that seems to break decisively with what Mowinckel terms the Reform prophets. This is partly because of what seems to be eccentric psychology on the part of this prophet, and partly because the language is priestly rather than the more familiar Torah-focused language. In any case, the "valley of dry bones" is a scenario permeated with the reality of the spirit.

At the very outset, the narrative begins:

> The hand of the Lord came upon me, and he brought me out by the spirit of the Lord, and set me down in the middle of a valley (v.1).

The language is peculiar, but in any case the whole of the (vision?) experience is initiated by the spirit. The whole of the experience is portrayed as somewhat surrealistic, as if the speaker claims that he transcended all conventional reality. We cannot, of course, determine if this is "psychology," as it has often been understood, or if it serves primarily as a rhetorical strategy.

As you know, the narrative proceeds to assert, "The bones are very dry," i.e., without any vitality. The overriding question which God puts is, "Can these bones live?" Is the question a ploy on God's part, or a test? Or is God bewildered and genuinely does not know? The prophet, whatever the intent of

God, is appropriately deferential, and reminds God that only God knows the future of the very dry bones. Any future for such dryness depends upon the intent and the power of God.

God answers God's own question, after the prophet refuses to answer. God announces what will be done:

> I will cause spirit to enter you and you shall live. I will lay sinews on you, and will cause flesh to come upon you, and cover you with skin, and put spirit in you, and you shall live (vv. 5-6).

The sequence of bones, sinews, flesh, and skin alerts us to the fact that this primitive physiology names bodily parts and so seems to require "breath." Thus the reality of spirit may here be biologically required, before it is taken to be theologically significant.

This verdict by Yahweh in vv. 5-6 is now implemented. In v. 8 there come sinews and flesh and skin...but no spirit. The *ruah* requires a second word of command from Yahweh:

> Come from the four winds O wind and breathe upon these slain, that they may have life (v. 9).

In this verse, God addresses spirit and commands spirit with an imperative, as an agent of Yahweh.

Finally in v. 18, the spirit comes into the bones

Gathering the Church in the Spirit ⚲

and they live! Thus, the little drama from v. 3 with dry bones to v. 9 with sinew, flesh, and skin to v. 18 with spirit. This is all accomplished by the two declarations of Yahweh, the first proposing a command, the second actually making a command, and then spirit obeying the command of God and causing life. We watch the inscrutable process from death to life.

In vv. 11-14 this remarkable scenario is now commented upon and interpreted. The bones are the whole house of Israel. The dryness is loss of hope, i.e., loss of any prospect for a future, completely cut off. Then the rhetoric escalates:

> I am going to open your graves and bring you back from your graves. O my people, I will bring you back to the land of Israel. You shall know I am Yahweh, when I open your graves and bring you up from your graves, O my people. I will put my spirit within you and you shall live. And I will place you on your own soil. Then you shall know that I, the Lord, have spoken and will act.[24]

The imagery is well known; but for all that, it is no less stunning. The rhetoric manages to hold together the imagery of homecoming and resurrection. Both are wrought by the spirit. Both are judged to be impossible, but both are made possible by the inscrutable wind of God.

This wind is God's self-starter in working a miracle, to bring the people of God to a new historical possibility, when all available possibilities have been nullified. The future of Israel now depends upon no conventional supports, for all those have vanished. Israel is indeed a "new thing" after it had entered its null point.[25] This radical vision knows nothing of Deuteronomic Torah, or of priestly promise, or of theodicy in the book of Job. It is as inexplicable as the blowing of the wind. Israel's new life in a new social circumstance is indeed *ex nihilo*, because "the force" will no more be explained than it will be harnessed.[26] Israel's life is completely taken out of its own hands, something unthinkable before the coming of the exile.

Ezekiel's problem, as always occurs in such arousals from nullity, is how to utter the unutterable, the reality of life-giving power that lies completely beyond control or summons. In chapter 1 of Ezekiel, concerning his great inaugural vision, one can see the prophet straining his language in order to talk about the massive splendor which overwhelms both a seemingly terminated Jerusalem and a seemingly empty exile.

Clearly the text tradition of Ezekiel struggles to articulate the overwhelmingness of what now moves Israel's disoriented, disestablished life. The prophet characterizes this stupendousness:

> Above the firmament over their heads there was the likeness of a throne, in appearance like sapphire; and seated about the likeness of a throne was a likeness as it were of a human form. And upward from what had the appearance of his loins I saw, as it were, gleaming bronze, like the appearance of fire enclosed round about and downward from

Gathering the Church in the Spirit ☩

what had the appearance of his loins I saw, as it were, the appearance of fire, and there was brightness round about him. Like the appearance of the bow that is in the cloud on the day of rain, so was the appearance of the brightness round about (1:26-28).

After the prophet finishes this lyrical witness, we still do not know. We do not know because it is all "like, likeness, appearance," and "as it were." But we do sense that everything has been surprisingly, unutterably changed, with no human initiative, but with full human attentiveness and responsiveness. This disoriented prophet bears witness to the spirit of newness. It is not difficult in our time and place to identify whole peoples who have "been brought back from the dead." This might include Blacks in South Africa, Palestinians in Israel, Catholics in Northern Ireland.

4. *Ezekiel 18:31, 36:27.* Two other texts from Ezekiel are important for our purposes and need to be related to each other. In Ezek. 18, the prophet offers a program of repentance for the wicked, which concerns the three "biggies" of idolatry, sexuality, and economics.[27] The intent of the chapter is to urge repentance. Thus, "Repent and turn from all your transgression. . .turn then and live" (vv. 30, 32). One other remarkable imperative is uttered: "Get yourselves a new heart and a new spirit." The imperative assumes that Israel is capable, by its resolve and choice, to operate in a wholly different spirit.

In 36:27, however, a very different stance is

taken by the prophet. This text is much later in the book, perhaps later in the evolution of this theological tradition. Now Israel's resources and capacity are spent and exhausted, and Israel has no adequate will for such deep repentance. Now, if there is to be anything different, it will be done by Yahweh for Israel, who on its own is helpless.[28]

The prophet speaks, on God's behalf, a series of sweeping promises:

> I will take you from the nations, and gather you from all the countries, and bring you into your own land. I will sprinkle clean water upon you, and you shall be clean from all your uncleannesses, and from all your idols I will cleanse you. A new heart I will give you; and a new spirit I will put within you; and I will remove from your body the heart of stone and give you a heart of flesh. I will put my spirit within you, and make you follow my statutes and be careful to observe my ordinances (vv. 24-27).

Whereas in chapter 18, Israel is to "make" a new spirit for itself, here it is Yahweh who will put a new heart and a new spirit, a new intention and a new capability that will make serious obedience possible, and will give well-being in the land:

> Then you shall live in the land that I gave to your ancestors; and you shall be my people, and I will be your God. I will save you from all uncleannesses, and I will summon the

grain and make it abundant and lay no famine upon you. I will make the fruit of the tree and the produce of the field abundant, so that you may never again suffer the disgrace of famine among the nations (vv. 28-30).

The spirit makes possible a new singular covenantal relation, thereby assuring God's solidarity with Israel, and God's restoration of the fruitfulness of all of creation. God, by God's spirit, will do for Israel what Israel cannot do for itself. In the contemporary U.S. Church, we seem to have problems of fatigue, doubt, controversy, and inadequacy that the church, by its own resolve cannot remedy. It may well be that God's spirit can do for the church what it cannot do for itself.

5. *Isaiah 61:1-7.* When we come to Isaiah 56-66 in perhaps 520 BCE, even Mowinckel agrees that we are into a quite different world of theological reality. (This text is often called "Third Isaiah" because it is dated later than Isaiah 1-39 and Isaiah 40-55.) Chapters 60-62 are an intense piece of poetry, straining to say something radically different. In 60:2 with the advent of light, we are told that "darkness shall cover the earth" and "thick darkness," which is perhaps an echo of the chaos in Gen. 1:2. In 61:1, as you know, our text begins with the spirit:

The spirit of the Lord God is upon me.

The language echoes 42:1 to which I have referred. In chapter 61, all the transformative actions now to be taken are to be taken by a human agent. But the human agent moves beyond self and self's interest and capacity to do what is humanly impossible. Yahweh, the one who sends the spirit, is the one who anoints and sends, who authorizes and dispatches, who turns loose in the world a human agent whom "the force" attends.

That human agent who has been "enspirited" now goes well beyond any conventional human possibility. That human agent is to enact the Jubilee Year anticipated as long ago as Leviticus 25:[29]

> . . .to bring good news to the oppressed,
> to bind up the broken hearted,
> to proclaim liberty to the captives,
>   and release to the prisoners;
> to proclaim the year of the Lord's favor,
>   and the day of vengeance of our God;
> to provide for those who mourn in Zion—
> to give them a garland instead of ashes,
> the oil of gladness instead of mourning,
> the mantle of praise instead of faint spirit (vv. 1b-3b).

There will be a general amnesty for the oppressed, the debt-prisoners, and thus an end to the economic system that has been enormously disordered and exploitative. There will be comfort, the comfort anticipated in 40:1, for all the sadness that has marked Judaism since 587 BCE. There will be garlands of rejoicing and praise, an end to mourning, faintness, and a moribund mood in a society that has run down and failed. The community that has paid double for its sins (40:2) and suffered double in its shame (61:7) will now receive a double portion of well-being, a full, rich, abundant, inexplicable gift, a massive reversal by this human agent who now has disproportionate authority to work a transformation.

And of course it is this text that becomes programmatic in Luke for the evangelical transformation of society:

> He unrolled the scroll and found the place where it was written: The spirit of the Lord is upon me... And he rolled up the scroll, gave it aback to the attendant, and sat down. The eyes of all in the synagogue were fixed on him. Then he began to say to them, "Today this scripture has been fulfilled in your hearing" (Luke 4:17-21).

> Go and tell John what you have seen and heard: the blind receive their sight, the lame walk, the lepers are cleansed, the deaf hear, the dead are raised, the poor have good news brought to them. And blessed is anyone who takes no offense at me (Luke 7:22-23).

The scandal is that this gift of power and well-being is given in unauthorized ways to an uncredentialed agent for an undeserving populace, a gift that will disrupt all socio-economic-political conventions, wrought by the spirit. In the Gospel narrative, the folk who heard Jesus read from the Isaiah text, and heard him apply the text to himself and his ministry, immediately recognized how dangerous was the claim. That is why they tried to kill him. They sensed, upon hearing, that in the life of Jesus power was being unleashed in the world that would call into question all of their old arrangements of power and advantage. The spirit in the life of Jesus is not a sweet, religious idea, but a revolutionary force which jeopardizes all that is old and disobedient in the world. And as politics is redefined by this utterance, so his listeners are also to think new theological thoughts. They become aware that spirit is not a religious property of theirs, but it is a force that brings newness which they do not welcome.

Mowinckel has also observed that in Isaiah 56-66, the great Moses-Joshua events are expressed as the work of the spirit:

> Where is the one who brought them up out of the sea
>> with the shepherds of his flock?
> Where is the one who put within them his holy *spirit*,
>> who caused his glorious arm
>> to march at the right hand of Moses,
>> who divided the waters before them
>> to make for himself an everlasting name,
>> who led them through the depths?
> Like a horse in the desert,
>> they did not stumble.
> Like cattle that go down into the valley,
>>> the *spirit* of the Lord gave them rest
> (63:llb-l4a).

The exodus is caused by the spirit which divides the waters, thus the same double entry as in Genesis 1, as "wind and spirit." Israel's entry into the land of rest, moreover, is given by the spirit of the Lord, in an anticipation of Psalm 23.[30] The spirit is the power of safety and well-being.

And now the poet speaks in an urgent, insistent lament:

> Where is the one who put within them his holy spirit?

Where now is the giver of spirit? In a disordered society, the community of faith waits for, remembers, and expects the spirit as a force which will change its public circumstance. When manageable life-supports fail, the community is driven to the spirit as the only source of its life. The church in our time seems to water down the claims of discipleship, especially as concerns obedience in political-economic matters. And in like manner, the church is rarely convinced that God can do "impossible things" in the world.

6. *Zechariah 4:6.* Just after the return from exile, perhaps in 520 BCE about the same time as III Isaiah (56-66), the prophet Zechariah anticipates the rebuilding of the temple and perhaps the restoration of Davidic political power. The language of the prophet moves toward apocalyptic, i.e., language that moves from historical expectation to other-worldly hope, which means of course that powerful hope for extrapolated newness is voiced. How is this so in a season of "small things" (Zech. 4:10)? Answer:

> Thus the word of the Lord to Zerubbabel: Not by might, not by power, but by my *spirit*, says the Lord of hosts.

Might and power are the best that human persons and agencies can muster. But might and power will not produce Israel's rehabilitation. How then? By my spirit. By my wind. By the "force" of God which neither Jewish despair nor imperial policy can thwart. The prophet, addressing the resisting empire, asserts,

> What are you O great mountain? Before Zerubbabel you shall become a plain; and he shall bring out the top stone amid shouts of "Grace, grace to it" (Zech. 4:7).

That sweeping assurance of Zechariah is reiterated by his contemporary, Haggai. There is a hope that Joshua the priest and Zerubbabel, heir to the Davidic throne, will restore well-being, but there is no viable, visible ground for hope. But Haggai countermands such despair:

> Who is left among you that saw this house in its former glory? How does it look to you now? Is it not in your sight as nothing? Yet now take courage, O Zerubbabel, says the Lord; take courage, O Joshua, son of Jehozadak, the high priest; take courage, all you people of the land, says the Lord; work, for I am with you, says the Lord of hosts, according to the promise that I made you when you came out of Egypt. My *spirit* abides among you; do not fear (Hag. 2:3-5).

The promise of the spirit is as old as the Exodus, whereby the waters were parted. And now that same "force" is assured for the Jews. Verse 6 continues:

> For thus says the Lord of Hosts: Once again, in a little while, I will shake the heavens and the earth and the sea and the dry land...I will fill this house with splendor, says the Lord of hosts (vv. 6-7).

The language is cosmic, the terms are apocalyptic. The prophet refuses to accent the limited, visible options. This community is invited to a revolutionary hope that is not world-escaping, but world-transforming. And that hope concerns precisely God's powerful spirit.

7. *Joel 2:28-29.* Finally I come to the appropriate conclusion of this inventory. The text is familiar to us:

> Then afterward
> > I will pour out my spirit on all flesh;
> > > your sons and your daughters shall prophesy,
> > > your old men shall dream dreams,
> > > and your young men shall see visions.
> > Even on the male and female slaves,
> > > in those days, I will pour out my spirit.

The "afterward" is after all "the troubles," by the gift, gift of the spirit everyone in the community—sons and daughters, young men and old, male and female, slaves and free, completely will have liberated imagination. The gift of the spirit is for prophecy, dreaming, and seeing visions, able to re-vision reality out beyond every debilitating convention. In commenting on this text, Hans Walter Wolff writes, "They confess a fearless confidence in the future acts of God on behalf of his people…[They express] prophetic certainty of the coming acts of God on behalf of his people.[31]

Much more may be said of this poetry, but I want to focus on the new ways of knowing that are made possible by the coming of the spirit. The gift of the spirit suggests that this community of old and young, free and slave, male and female, is not so committed to the visible and the given, but is ener-gized to entertain a genuine and profound alternative to what the world regards as settled. Indeed, the faithful, singing praises to God, host a concreteness about the future that is more trustworthy than what is seen or controlled, for what is seen and in hand is in the end immobilizing and deadening.

You are, moreover, as aware as am I that it is this Joel text that becomes the theme text for Peter's great Pentecost sermon in Acts 2:14-36. In this ser-mon Peter takes his own moment of history to be the "afterward" of Joel 2:28. He imagines that under the imperative of the spirit the future of the world in the resurrection is more reliable than the closed, set-tled world of the empire. That strange gift in Acts 2 sets in motion this odd, inexplicable tale of a church that turns the world upside down (Acts 17:6), there-by confounding the rulers of this age.

Now I am not at all sure that these are the right texts about which we should be speaking. They are in any case an extraordinary array of texts that envision a force set loose in the world, that none of the assumed givens can finally withstand.

From these texts we may notice several recurring accents which bear upon the present crisis of the church:

1. The spirit causes human agents to act afresh, in ways they had not intended or envisioned.

2. The work of the human agent thus "spirited" is to transform reality toward justice.

3. The "spirited" human agent need not be "attractive," but only faithful and capable of risk-taking.

4. The agent works for the sake of the whole community.

5. The spirit does the work of restoration which the community cannot do for itself.

6. The spirit works in ways the world does not expect or even recognize.

7. The spirit invites daring acts of imagination

III.
A Church Invaded By the Spirit

It is this move from *word* to *spirit* that I suggest befits the church in a society transitioning to a disordered sort of pluralism in which old certitudes of knowledge and power are deeply at risk. You see, in the world of Israel before 587 BCE, things were settled and ordered enough to permit "word theology." There were prophets who spoke the word. There were kings to be addressed. There were courts and temples where the word was sounded and uttered. There was the apparatus of the "divine council" which gave a word so credentialed that it could be said, "Thus saith the Lord."[32] In exile and beyond exile, however, those settled ways of powerful utterance were no longer adequate or credible. A more desperate, disordered situation required a more wild, undomesticated mode of life exposed to the staggering, invasive "force" of God which blows where it will. Informed by Mowinckel, I suggest ours is a time like that, when the church cannot assume institutional supports, but is freed and required to be open in ways unfettered and unsupported.

I do not want to contrast too casually a faith centered in "the word" versus one centered in "the spirit," though we must face the growing sense that word theology does tend to conspire with the Western male domination that proceeds in "reasonable" ways. Nor do I want to put matters so that the theology of the Second Person of the Trinity is in tension with Third Person theology. I do, however, have the sense that the tight control of theology by reference to Jesus over the freedom of God's spirit, of Christological control over pneumatology, may be a Western political commitment. Such a commitment tends, perhaps unintentionally, to establish privilege and advantage, whereas disestablished persons cannot count on such privilege and must be more available for the wild disruptiveness of "the force." That is, the way we organize theology tends to reflect our situation of relative power or relative need.

I am not at all sure how to proceed to the next phase of my argument, nor how radically we might want to push these seeds of rethinking. Let me hint at five dimensions of church life and practice which may suggest a parallel to the disestablished exilic Judaism which focuses on the spirit of Yahweh.

1. It occurs to me that under the aegis of the spirit, the possible relations of *church* and *culture* are much less precise and much more porous than our usual models, so that the enlivening, transformative spirit may turn up in all kinds of places and modes that lie outside the control of the church and beyond the horizon of the church.

Specifically, I suggest that issues concerning the relationship of faith and culture in the future may well pay great attention to the arts as a way in which the edges of pain and possibility in society come to availability. It is no accident that what has been called "the work of the spirit" is now much more likely to be taken as "imagination." John Thiel has written of "a pneumatology of the imagination" that not only exposes and diagnoses, but also anticipates and construes new possibilities.[33] By this phrase, Thiel means that the spirit (in Greek, *pneuma*) may be and often is the enlivening power of imagination. Thus the imagining done in art which often seems threatening may be the leading of the spirit to help us envision the world in new ways. It is clear enough that poetry, novels, stories, music, and paintings may describe wretchedness and cruelty and despair. But art, like dream, may also move forward to conjure new configurations of reality not yet available in more cognitive modes.[34] Thus it is not accidental that much of the most compelling and poignant art comes from the wounded and marginated who construe reality alternatively. This means that the breaks toward God's will and purpose are not always channeled through or packaged in ways habitual to the church, but the church may come late to discern the breaking in of the spirit in the life of the world.

Such a turn in theological categories may put the church at the edge of society, as a belated discerner and observer of such actions of the spirit. The church may catch up with the newness wrought by God in the world. The church has no monopoly on controllable or infallible categories, and can increasingly lower its resistant voice about where God is doing newness. I do not want to make easy connections, but I submit that this mode of discernment may be hinted at with the flurry over "sophia" in recent times.[35] This enterprise may be a way in which the workings of God break through our tightly understood Christological discernment. Much of the church can hardly tolerate the notion that the spirit may be at work in the world in ways ill-fitting the categories which we assign to the power of God. But God is not tamed by the church and may lead us to go where we had not intended.

2. I suggest we may need to rethink what a *spirit-filled piety* might look like. It may place much more accent on undomesticated energy than it does upon docile civility. It may take on a mood of disruption and abrasion rather than a peaceable kind of conformity, because the spirit-filled are often awkward in the ways of the world. It need not, however, be only disruptive and abrasive. It may also be a mode of life which is transformative, constructive, and conciliatory, but in an active stance which breaks vicious cycles.

Three aspects of piety are pertinent for a church in which its social hegemony has been lost. First, its *liturgy* must be bold, so as to counter grief and despair. Very much establishment liturgy serves primarily as social maintenance. If it is grief and despair that rob the church of missional energy, then liturgy must be directed precisely against those temptations. In the face of grief, liturgy must penetrate denial over loss, in order to express the grief as sadness, rage, and a sense of abandonment. Such protests, when finally voiced, may readily move to promises which are specific and which move well beyond common social expectation. A liturgic enterprise of rage and vision is a model very different from an accent upon guilt and repentance which characterizes most establishment liturgy.

The *sacramental* dimension of such liturgy is

important to recover. Of course sacraments can also be made into gestures of social stability. But the prayer for the spirit to come upon the waters of baptism and the prayer at the center of Eucharist which asks God's spirit to come upon the bread and the wine mean that the moving, surging spirit of God is central to sacraments for a church given over to transformation. Each of the sacraments is understood as a vehicle whereby God's spirit works newness.

Second, piety in much of our church tradition is focused upon a kind of morality which sorts things out in terms of a "safe" goodness. In a kept church, the issues of morality have been greatly reduced to matters of private conduct and, more specifically sexuality, which in turn has nurtured an excessive scrupulosity. Now I agree that responsible, disciplined conduct is a *sine qua non* for a church in a context of disestablishment. But personal conduct cannot be the be-all and end-all of "morality." Rather the moral practice of a spirit-driven church is the freedom to transcend such scrupulosity, in order to challenge the social "givens" that block the emergence of genuine human life.

The commands of the gospel are indeed urgent. A church without a social hegemony to support, however, can learn to reread the commands of the gospel through social criticism, to see that they emancipate the spirit-filled church to address orders and principalities that violate the liberating, healing, caring promises of the gospel. "Morality" in such a church has less to do with purity (though I do not advocate impurity) than it has to do with energy, courage, and freedom for social transformation.[36]

Third, the piety of such a church surely includes *personal prayer and devotion.* Such a practice for believers in a posture of openness, however, is not prayer and pondering out of a given order in which we are placed. It is rather prayer and pondering precisely in the yet inchoate coming kingdom, in order to anticipate and receive gifts where they are given, to discern signs of its coming, and to position ourselves for its enactment among us.

In its *liturgical-sacramental, moral,* and *devotional aspects,* this piety is a waiting, expectant, receiving posture of faith. That means, it must be genuinely alternative to every settled reflection upon the *status quo.* In his rich and suggestive report on Jewish devotional life, Jacob Neusner proposes that the rituals of Jewish faith are supports for acts of imagination, whereby one may imagine that he or she is a Jew.[37] Indeed, says Neusner, being a Jew is fundamentally an act of imagination. If one does not so imagine, Jewishness evaporates, and one disappears into the landscape of assimilation into the larger culture. In post-establishment Christianity, one must imagine oneself to be a Christian who has "renounced the vainglories of the world" (thus baptism) and who "proclaims the Lord's death until he comes" (thus Eucharist). That is, one must each day imagine oneself to be Christian.

3. It is more difficult, but no less urgent, to think about *spirit-filled polity,* which among other things, is to ask about denominationalism when the denominations have become relatively weak and

marginal. Here I tread very lightly, because I am not at all sure that we know how to think connectionally without the power of domination at our disposal.

I suspect we shall have to think of drastic ways to overcome the bureaucratic mind-set and the corporation model that tend to move in terms of large budgets, programs, organizational charts, and full-time, life-time staff. Or perhaps our denominational structures in these extreme, self-conscious forms turn out to be imitators of worldly procedures that are not congenial to the way the church must live its life, short of hegemonic responsibility and support.

I have in mind a minimalist notion of church polity which does not spend so much of its energy on punctilious governance, personnel, location, and large policy positions which occasionally enable the church, but which work more often to immobilize the church in divisiveness and anger.

The most I can suggest are conversation starters:

- One colleague said that what denominations did before the big bureaucratic time was to dispatch missionaries and produce curriculum. That is all, he said. Such functions might be minimal and are increasingly local and potentially ecumenical in locale.

- Hans Walter Wolff, when asked about how the Confessing Church in Germany ordered and sustained its life, said, "We did two things. We wrote lots of letters and studied the Bible."

- Tip O'Neill, former Speaker of the U.S. House of Representatives, said, "All politics is local." Perhaps all "Church is local." Indeed, the ecumenical vision is "all in each place." I sense that many of our young are watching to see what we intend and risk and imagine locally.

- Martin Marty, a Lutheran theologian and a foremost church historian, has proposed that denominations are like extended families:

    The bottom line: denominations don't define us: They are like families. Even extended families don't address and settle things from a distance; they improvise locally, nuclearly, in the light of family tradition, as they welcome new light from wherever. Then they link up for reunions, to work together, to fight and then, also, to love.[38]

    Extended families must not take themselves with such seriousness.

- Stephen Toulmin, a current political philosopher, proposes that modernity had pretensions and universalizing ambitions it worked out by writing, universal claims, general axioms, and timeless essences.[39] The move to post-modernity, however, is a move toward the oral, the concrete, the local, the timely.[40] In making such a move with confidence and freedom, it may be enough.

- In Montgomery, Alabama, if I have my numbers correct, there were eleven Presbyterian congregations, eight of whom left the PCUS for the Presbyterian Church in America. The other three, plus two new ones, have been driven together by their suffering and abuse. Now they know each other, care about each other, identify with each other, and are increasingly prepared to do mission together. Quite clearly, the primary bonding among them is not structural polity, but the substance of faith and the cost of mission. And perhaps if there were only one such congregation left in Montgomery, it might even make common cause with a like-spirited non-Presbyterian congregation. It has been known to happen.

I would not say that our much structured church life defies the spirit. But our usual ordering of the church cannot make it easy for the spirit. What if there were simplification enough that discipleship in obedience bound people to sacraments and hymns? And those who could not join "the issues" could in the meantime pay and pray, in order to maintain an infrastructure of local life. The losses in such a "light" notion of the church would be considerable, but not as great if we recognize that most of the glory of dominance has already departed from the church. In fact, the evangelical issues in our society are too urgent for the disproportionate energy that tight polity requires. *The polity questions seem to me not so much how to "maintain decency and order" but how to become energized for urgent mis-*

sion, with enough openness in a church to use many gifts among those who will never agree on anything.

The spirit may call the church to new forms of being that are not Episcopal, Presbyterian, or Congregational, but more like a network of grapevine and associations of all those baptized into a dangerous identity. Such a possibility of course is not absent when we ponder the early church in its work of contagion in a super-power empire. It is my impression that except for mood and ethos, *most of the things we imagine to be definitive and distinctive for a particular church in fact are not,* but we continue to think so because of our isolation and ignorance.[41]

4. From the crisis of polity, of course, comes the *crisis of policy.* It is at this point that the church most radically evidences its pluralism, i.e., a myriad of competing voices, in which folk are coming and going to find a church that will voice "their truth" and fence out "another truth" which they find to be false. Clearly many view the emergence of pluralism as an unutterable misfortune, hoping to recover what is called an earlier "consensus" and "coherence." Those who are accustomed to announce the truth for all the others yearn for a time when the truth was so readily announceable. Such large-scale announcements of truth are debilitating in a church that on many fronts clearly does not know the mind of Christ. Of course a church with potential for domination cannot afford to waffle. It must be right, or appear to be right, even if the winners have only 54 percent of opinion.

But a church made up of exiles inevitably has

many diverse notions about how to posture faith over-against a dominant culture that now largely ignores the noise of the church. That is, if the church is not taken so seriously by culture, it can afford to acknowledge in honest ways its own uncertain pluralism. When the church was important to upholding public value, the church had to be careful and "prudent." Now in its new situation, the church may take more risks in speaking the truth. These several postures may be arranged on a continuum of *accommodation* to society and *confrontation* with society, and we shift on that continuum from issue to issue. Such a church might more honestly admit that we, most of us, are ambiguous, ambivalent, and double-minded, and do not want to decide. And so we pray, "Deliver us from the time of trial," or as we say "lead us not into temptation, but deliver us from evil," the temptation to sell out and give up our baptism.

The spirit-filled church in Acts did not duck issues, but it also did not pronounce on every crisis issue that came along. Moreover, in the Old Testament there are a variety of strategies for being faithful in exile, ranging from confrontation to scribal "resident aliens," to eager apocalyptists to wisdom teachers to royal courtiers. [42] The compromise which became the canon suggests that those exiles did not drive each other out of the community. *They stayed with the core story, and allowed many forms of faith and many practices of life to exist together.*

But such an openness requires the conviction that others (who seem completely wrong) are living in good faith, may also be led by the spirit, and must

Gathering the Church in the Spirit ♥

be prayed for, in their very odd form of witness. Hans Frei, a recent important theologian at Yale, speaks of a "generous orthodoxy"

> which would have in it an element of liberalism—a voice like the *Christian Century*—and an element of evangelicalism—voice of *Christianity Today*.[43]

If the church is able to trust the spirit, it can afford to be generous in its orthodoxy and in its notion of right living. And indeed it must be generous, if in our pluralism beyond hegemony, we do not wish to excommunicate all but ourselves.

5. In the end, what matters is not so much a *practice toward society*, a *piety*, a *polity* or a *policy*. *What finally matters decisively is a spirit-filled faith, a conviction that the core narrative of the gospel has quite concrete credibility, out of which we are prepared to act and toward which we are prepared to witness.* Such a preparedness for action and witness is not so urgent in a pre-exilic situation in which things hang together on their own. But now, dethroned and displaced, this action and witness matter urgently, and we are feed for them. Faith—not to say doctrine—is relatively simple. It asserts trust in this other character who in great weakness enters our life in powerful acts of surprise which transform and heal. The new situation in a post-hegemonic church is to see if our walk and our talk can be put together in freshly compelling ways. Such a conviction, such a passion, when made concretely, is unexpectedly powerful. It is of course enormously risky and problematic as well.

IV.
Led By the Spirit, Unfettered and Unafraid

This post-hegemonic church, dethroned and displaced, now more than in any recent time, has "strength unequal to its task." If I am right in appealing to Mowinckel that pre-587 Israel was *word-oriented* and that post-587 Israel was *spirit-compelled*, then I raise questions about the juxtaposition of word and spirit.

I suggest three possible ways of thinking about the tension between this pair of theological labels.

1. Can the church move out of its posture of focusing on the "absolute" WORD in Jesus, which has assumed privileged certitude, which is found by many to be unhelpfully authoritarian? Some recent critics of patriarchy, among whom I hope I qualify, suggest that patriarchal, phallocentric power and logocentric authority are all of a piece. I do not wish to do a Freudian analysis of that suggested convergence. I observe only that a logocentric church has been busy these many centuries, under leadership of males like myself, getting the words right for a single articulation of truth which has become orthodoxy capable of reassurance, but which was also capable of condemning and causing disproportionate suffering.

Those kinds of certitudes, powerfully cast in treasured words, will no doubt continue to be important to us, even if they have been to some extent imposed. But those formulations are not now as adequate as they once were. It is evident, I take it, that the feminization of ministry has introduced into the life of the church other modes of communication and certitude that are more open and nurturing and even suggestive of the move of the spirit. This is for the church to ponder in a society where old-line logo-authority does not hold very well.

If the church moves from its long-established logocentric posture, it means that it gives up something of its conventional modes of authority and certitude. This does not mean, of course, that a church ceases its proclamation and transformative utterance. It does mean, however, that such proclamation and utterance do not happen characteristically in a hard, absolutist voice that assumes it can speak so absolutely because it is allied with the absolutizing powers of the world. In place of such conventional assumptions, the mode, mood, tone, and posture of the church become the voice of uncredentialed power, passion, and resilience. Such a church does not utter universal claims, but bears witness to the odd, concrete, and unexpected ways in which "the force" has been evidenced in ways that defy all of our symmetrical, domesticated categories.

2. Can the church rethink the *filioquy clause*? The phrase "filioquy clause" refers to an important and very old controversy in the church concerning a phrase in the Nicene creed. The full form of the creed says that the spirit "proceeds from the Father *and the Son*." The phrase "and the Son" in Greek has the word *filius* (Son) and the conjunction *que*

(and), thus the phrase *filioquy* refers to the phrase "and the Son." The Western Roman church (of which we are a part) has always insisted on using this phrase, "and the Son," insisting that the spirit derives *from the Son*, and therefore must look like and act like "the Son." The Eastern church has rejected the phrase and insisted that the spirit need not act and look like the Son, but may bear only the marks of the Father.

What seems a very small grammatical debate is in fact a discussion of enormous importance, because the abandonment of the clause permits the acknowledgment that "God the Father" may do things in the world that do not look all that much like "Jesus." In current discussion, both Jurgen Moltmann and Douglas Hall, distinguished Reformed theologians, mount a criticism of the phrase, because it has caused a restrictive view of where God is at work in the world.

I am not a systematic theologian, leave alone a historian of doctrine. The Western commitment to *filioquy* has completely subordinated the spirit to the son, the *wind* to the *word*, thus making the spirit subordinate to the logocentric claims upon which I have already commented. That is, in practice "the force" is categorically defined by the confession of Christ. Douglas Hall comments, "The spirit is bound hand and foot to the doctrine of the 'second person.'"[44]

I am sure that I do not grasp all of the theological problems in the Eastern alternative. It is in any case a consequence of the Eastern formulation (without that clause) that the spirit is confessed to be alive and visible in the ways of the world, apart from any Christological claim. Thus all of creation is known to be an arena for the work of the spirit. Now it may be that all such is possible with the *filioquy* when a high view of logos is affirmed in trinitarian thinking. But in practice it has not worked out that way.

Through the absence of the clause, it is possible to acknowledge that the creator God has unleashed God's own life-giving "force" everywhere in God's creation, in many modes and cultural forms, well beyond the confessional horizons of the church's Christology. The consequence is that the church recognizes its own theological position as a marginated witness to the great transformative actions wrought by God's spirit. Thus the absence of *filioquy* has the practical consequence of minimizing the church's authority in defining and identifying the liberating threat and healing gift of the spirit.

There are moves in this direction in current theological thinking, of which we may identify:

a) Chung Hyun Kyung at the World Council Assembly in Canberra shocked and stunned many with her affirmation that God's spirit of liberation may well surge beyond the old bounds of the church and weary Christlandom.[45]

b) Konrad Raiser of the World Council of Churches can write about a "paradigm shift" and propose an "ecumenism of solidarity" in place of an "ecumenism of domination," an ecumenism that assumes no Christian privilege, but attends to the work of the spirit in bringing to the world a genuine human community.[46]

c) Jurgen Moltmann insists upon denying the *filioquy*, but guards his claim by the affirmation that the spirit proceeds from the Father, who is "always *the Father of the Son*."[47] Moltmann, however, stops short of articulating the ecclesial consequences of his argument.

d) Douglas Hall, as distinct from Moltmann, insists that the clause be retained.[48] Then, however, he continues, "But it is one thing to insist that the spirit proceeds from the father *and the son*, and something else to say that the spirit must conform to our Christologies!"

e) My colleague at Columbia Theological Seminary, George Stroup, has helped me with reference to Moltmann and Leonardo Boff. Stroup has suggested his worry "that questioning the *filioquy* clause is worked out not primarily on the basis of the Bible's land theology, but on the basis of their social and political agenda."[49] Stroup of course recognizes that such pressures were also operative in the formulation of the classic phrase in the first case. I do not flinch from the impingement of socio-political factors in this issue, because that is precisely our missional agenda. The question to be faced is precisely whether the church in a social setting of intense pluralism does not in its formulation shift its weight to the work of the spirit, which does not always look or sound like "Christian stuff," or produce consequences that strike us as true-blue Christian.

3. What can the church in such a culture of transition like ours learn from the book of Acts? I am no restorationist, i.e., one who believes that the sim-

Gathering the Church in the Spirit

ple, ancient church can be recovered in present context, and I have no romantic notion of a destructured church. It may be, however, that in a pluralistic culture where the church is increasingly dislodged from prominence, and its old modes of impact and domination are diminished, we may learn afresh from that model of church. Indeed, I suggest that how the church lives and acts in the Book of Acts is not unlike Israel in its painful exile, where appeal to the spirit had to be made. I cite the following:

a) The account of the church in Acts is about the disruptive, generative, originary power of the spirit, in a society that assumed no newness could disrupt the authority of the "super-power" (Rome).

b) While the narrative of Acts focuses upon the force of the spirit, the actions taken are characteristically those of emboldened human agents, seized and compelled by one beyond themselves, by "the force." It is a narrative of the unafraid.

c) The thematic quote from Joel 2:28-32 (Acts 2:17-21), concerns old and young, slave and free, male and female, who dream dreams and see visions. The quote is set in a social context in which alternative possibilities are given to the church by the spirit. And this for and in a society regimented and managed by technique, which intends to co-opt all visions and dreams. Thus our "pneumatology of imagination" is operative in this defining narrative of the church.

d) The church in Acts, of course, is no stranger to controversy. But the vision of Peter in Acts 10:11-16 and the decision of Acts 15:19 places the church venturesomely on the side of generous grace and inclusiveness, which seemed to violate all old, treasured protocols. No doubt there is a linkage between the "force" and the kind of practical, pastoral decisions that were made to give the church its awesome future.

e) The church is persuasive and bold in the face of the authorities, refusing to be silent, cowed, or accommodated to the policy-makers (Acts 20-24). There is something unfettered and unguarded about this church, even though the sign-off of the narrative in 28:26-27 has to do with the resistance of dull hearts, ears hard of hearing, and eyes shut.

The reconsideration of the church in a society where old forms and old privilege are in doubt has enormous import. It is entirely plausible, given our past, that the very "force" to whom we may bear new witness is the very force which compels and permits this reconsideration. Spirit-language is one way in which our people have uttered the unutterable, which lies outside all of our conventional, more congenial, controlled categories.

Thus the burden of my argument is that the church in the United States stands at a pivotal moment of opportunity that concerns pastors and lay folk alike. This moment may be taken as one of failure, discouragement and fear, as the church no longer has the "clout" it had for many centuries after it became "official." It may well be, however, that our faithful response to this moment is not one of fear, anxiety, and regret. It is possible that in this moment, the spirit of God is moving the church away from old assumptions, old practices, and old patterns of power and authority into a new season of power, energy, fidelity, and mission.

It is my urging that we entertain this second alternative sense of ourselves. In light of such an affirmation, people in the church are summoned to reconsider that the claims of the gospel be taken with new, joyful seriousness. The truth of the gospel—that there is strength in weakness, that life is stronger than death, that neighbor counts in the reign of God—is a claim that now is urgent, as it has not been for a long time. What is now permitted and required is that baptized people think and act afresh about this faith we claim. And as we think and act so, we may find new gifts given by the spirit, gifts of freedom, energy, courage, and imagination. What might possibly eventuate as this "force" comes among us is "all things new."

Walter Brueggemann
Columbia Theological Seminary

Notes

1. On Israel's transition to monarchy, see Frank S. Frick, *The Formation of the State in Ancient Israel: A Survey of Models and Theories* (Sheffield: JSOT Press, 1985) and Norman K. Gottwald (ed.), *Social Scientific Criticism of the Hebrew Bible and Its Social World: The Israelite Monarchy, Semeia 37* (1986).

2. Thus Arnold J. Toynbee, *A Study of History*, notoriously treats ancient Israel as a minor sub-set in the history of "Syriac Civilization." It is clear, however, that Toynbee cannot finally dispose of peculiar Jewishness. See *A Study of History XII* (New York: Oxford University Press, 1961) 209-17, 483-88 and *passim*. The matter is very different for Eric Voeglin, *Order and History I: Israel and Revelation* (Baton Rouge: Louisiana State University Press, 1956).

3. Concerning the exile, the standard works are Peter R. Ackroyd, *Exile and Restoration: A Study of Hebrew Thought of the Sixth Century B.C.* (Philadelphia: Westminster,

1968), E. Janssen, *Juda in der Exilszeit: Ein Beitrag zur Frage der Entstehung des Judentums* (FRLANT 69; Gottingen: Vandenhoeck and Reprecht, 1956), Ralph W. Klein, *Israel in Exile: A Theological Interpretation* (OBT; Philadelphia: Fortress, 1979), and Daniel L. Smith, *The Religion of the Landless: The Social Context of the Babylonian Exile* (Indianapolis: Meher-Stone, 1989).

4. Walter Brueggemann, "Rethinking Church Models Through Scripture," *Theology Today 48*[2] (July, 1991) 128-138, "Preaching to Exiles," *Journal for Preachers* XVI[4] (Pentecost, 1993) 3-15, and "Cadences Which Redescribe: Speech Among Exiles," *Journal for Preachers* XVII[3] (Easter, 1994) 10-17.

5. Brueggemann, "Preaching to Exiles," 4.

6. *Ibid.*, 3.

7. *Ibid.*

8. For example, John Burton, *Conflict: Resolution and Prevention* (New York: St. Martin's Press, 1990) 13-14, writes: "Societies, and Western industrial societies

in particular, have moved to a stage of ambiguity and confusion in social controls that can only be described as a mess."

9. Christopher R. Seitz, *Theology and Conflict: Reactions to the Exile in the Book of Jeremiah* (BZAW 176; Berlin: Walter de Gruyter, 1989).

10. For a case in point, see Walter Brueggemann, "A Second Reading of Jeremiah after the Dismantling," *Ex Auditu* 1 (1985) 156-68.

11. Thus for example, Max Stackhouse, *Christian Century* after acknowledging the reality and crisis of pluralism, urges that we should all return to "Catholic faith," which Stackhouse himself knows best. J. Cheryl Exum, *Fragmented Women: Feminist (Sub) versions of Biblical Narratives* (JSOT Supp. 163; Sheffield: Sheffield Academic Press, 1993).

12. My impression is that the recent series of seven books on the history of contemporary Presbyterianism, edited by John Mulder and Louis Weeks, inclines to yearn for a consensus that is now gone. And where that consensus has disappeared, there is a propensity

to view that as a decline from "better" times.

13. Rainer Albertz, *Religionsgeschicht Israels in alttestamentlicher Zeit 1 and 2* (Gottingen: Vandenhoeck & Reprecht, 1992) has taken as the defining reality of Israel's religion the fact of pluralism. He shows, moreover, that the canon is itself a work of compromise among competing voices.

14. For a general introduction to the issues, see Terence E. Fretheim, *Deuteronomic History* (Interpreting Biblical Texts; Nashville: Abingdon Press, 1983).

15. In addition to the work of Albertz cited in n. 13, see Robert B. Coote and David Robert Ord, *In the Beginning: Creation and the Priestly History* (Minneapolis: Fortress Press, 1991).

16. The anthropological work of Mary Douglas has been especially important for an understanding of the need for order in the Priestly tradition. See for example, Mary Douglas, "The Forbidden Animals in Leviticus," JSOT 59 (1993) 3-23. See also Peter J. Kearney, "Creation and Liturgy: The

Redaction of Ex. 25-40," ZSW 89 (1977) 375-87.

17. On the social location and function of Job, see Samuel Terrien, "Job as Sage," *The Sage in Israel and the Ancient Near East* ed. by John G. Gammie and Leo Perdue (Winona Lake: Eisenbrauns, 1990) 231-242, and Rainer Albertz, "The Sage and Pious Wisdom in the Book of Job: The Friends' Perspective," *ibid.*, 243-61. Concerning the utilization of older forms in Job, see Claus Westermann, *The Structure of the Book of Job: A Form-Critical Analysis* (Philadelphia: Fortress Press, 1981) and Katherine J. Dell, *The Book of Job as Sceptical Literature* (BZAW 197; Berlin: Walter de Gruyter, 1991).

18. See Gerhard von Rad, *Old Testament Theology II* (San Francisco: Harper and Row, 1965) 220-77, Walter Brueggemann, *Hopeful Imagination: Prophetic Voices in Exile* (Philadelphia: Fortress Press, 1986), and Albertz, *Religionsgeschichte 2*, 427-59.

19. See the helpful summary of pluralism as offered by Albertz, *ibid.*, 467.

20. On the political dimension of canonization,

see Frank Kermode, *Forms of Attention* (Chicago: University of Chicago Press, 1985) 67-93, who has written about the formal process of canonization under the cunning rubric, "Disentangling Knowledge from Opinion."

21. Sigmund Mowinckel, "'The Spirit' and the 'Word' in the PreExilic Reforming Prophets," JBL LIII (1934) 199-227.

22. See Carroll Stuhlmueller, *Creative Redemption in DeuteroIsaiah* (Analecta Biblica 43; Rome: Biblical Institute Press, 1970).

23. On such a nuance to the phrase, see Claus Westermann, *Genesis 1-11, A Commentary* (Minneapolis: Augsburg Publishing House, 1984) 166.

24. Walther Zimmerli, *Ezekiel 2* (Hermeneia; Philadelphia, 1983) 262-64, observes that the phrasing "my spirit" is different from most of the other uses of spirit and indicates the decisive, transformative intention of the divine oracle.

25. The phrase "null point" refers to the terminology employed by Walther Zimmerli,

"Plans for Rebuilding After the Catastrophe of 587," *I Am Yahweh* (Atlanta: John Knox Press, 1982). He refers variously to "the blessing of the nadir" (p. 111), "the opportunity of point zero" (p. 115), and "the blessing of point zero" (p. 133).

26. Concerning *ex nihilo*, Hans Heinrich Schmid, "Rechtfertigung als Schopfingsgecchen," *Rechtfertigang* ed. by Johannes Friedrich et. al. (Gottingen: Vandenhoeck & Reprecht, 1976) 412, has proposed that a) *creatio ex nihilio*, b) resurrection from the dead, and c) justification by grace function in close connection to each other. This is evident here as the themes converge (cf. Rom. 4:17).

27. On this important chapter, see Paul Joyce, *Divine Initiative and Human Response in Ezekiel* (JSOT Supp. 51; Sheffield: Sheffield Academic Press, 1989) chapter 3.

28. On chapter 36, see Brueggemann, *Hopeful Imagination*, 69-87.

29. Concerning the Jubilee Year, see John Howard Yoder, *The Politics of Jesus: Viit Agnus Noster* (Grand Rapids: Eerdmans, 1972) 34-40, 64-77, and *passim*, and Sharon H. Ringe, *Jesus, Liberation, and the Biblical*

Jubilee: Images for Ethics and Christology (OBT; Philadelphia: Fortress Press, 1985).

30. With reference to Psalm 78:19, David Noel Freedman has suggested that Psalm 23 refers to the wilderness sojourn. We are able to note a convergence of motifs related to Israel's memory.

31. Hans Walter Wolff, *Joel and Amos* (Hermeneia; Philadelphia: Fortress Press, 1977) 66-67.

32. On the "divine council," see E. Theodore Mullen, Jr., *The Divine Council in Canaanite and Early Hebrew Literature* (Chicago: Scholars Press, 1980).

33. John E. Theil, *Imagination and Authority: Theological Authorities in the Modern Tradition* (Minneapolis: Fortress Press, 1991) 213. Bernhard Anderson, *The Living Word of the Bible* (Philadelphia: Westminster Press, 1979) 13-35, deals with the authority of scripture under the rubric "Word of Imagination." He suggests that the work of the spirit is intimately linked to the exercise of imagination. This is a remarkable statement by Anderson, long before "imagination" became faddish in hermeneutical conversation.

34. Paul Ricoeur, *Freud and Philosophy: An Essay in Interpretation* (New Haven: Yale University Press, 1970) has suggested that dreams are not only "archaeology" as Freud understood, but that one can also "dream toward."

35. I refer to the ecumenical feminist meeting in Minneapolis in January, 1994, which has been so unsettling to some in the church. Part of the unsettling is because, using an ancient church tradition, God was addressed as "*sophia*."

36. On the tension between "purity" and "liberation" see Fernando Belo, *A Materialist Reading of the Gospel of Mark* (Maryknoll, N.Y.: Orbis Books, 1981), and see the reference to Mary Douglas in n. 16.

37. Jacob Neusner, *The Enchantments of Judaism: Rites of Transformation from Birth Through Death* (New York: Basic Books, 1987). On p. 214, he writes, "*We are Jews through the power of our imagination*" (Neusner's italics).

38. Martin Marty, "Young Lutherans' Guide to Sex," *Christian Century* (November 10, 1993) 1143.

39. Stephen Toulmin, *Cosmopolis: The Hidden Agenda of Modernity* (New York: The Free Press, 1990) 30-35.

40. *Ibid.*, 186-92.

41. Will Herberg, *Protestant, Catholic, Jew: An Essay in American Religious Sociology* (New York: Doubleday, 1955) has shown the remarkable homogenization of religious tradition in the United States. It would be relatively easy, in my judgment, to tell a parallel story of the homogenization of U.S. Protestant denominations, not brought about simply by accommodation to cultural forces, but also by ecumenical intentionality.

42. Daniel Smith, *The Religion of the Landless*, has characterized some of the diverse strategies required in the exile, which are evidenced in the literature.

43. Hans Frei, "Response to [C F H Henry] 'Narrative Theology: An Evangelical Appraisal,'" *Trinity Journal* 8 NS (1987) 21-24. I am grateful to Charles Campbell for this reference.

44. Douglas John Hall, *Thinking the Faith: Christian Theology in a North American Context* (Minneapolis: Augsburg Fortress, 1989) 105.

45. Chung Hyun Kyung, "Come Holy Spirit—Renew the Whole Creation," *Signs of The Spirit: Official Report, Seventh Assembly, Canberra, Australia, 7-20 February 1991* ed. by Michael Kinnamon (Grand Rapids: Eerdmans, 1991) 37-47.

46. Konrad Raiser, *Ecumenism in Transition: A Paradigm Shift in the Ecumenical Movement?* (Geneva: WCC Publications, 1991) 63.

47. Jurgen Moltmann, *The Trinity and the Kingdom: The Doctrine of God* (San Francisco: Harper & Row, 1981) 182-185.

48. Hall, *Thinking the Faith*, 105, n. 50.

49. George Stroup in private communication. I am grateful to Stroup for helping me think through this issue.

For Group Discussion

S E S S I O N   I

1. View Session I of the video presentation.
2. Is Exile an appropriate metaphor for the church's situation today? Give reasons for your answer.
3. What evidence do you see of the Exile of the contemporary mainline congregation?
4. In what ways is your own church in a state of Exile?

S E S S I O N   I I

1. View Session II of the video presentation.
2. What is the biblical meaning of "Spirit"?
3. What different shades of meaning do you find in the seven texts cited by the author? Compare your answers with his summary at the end of section II.
4. In light of these interpretations of the Spirit, where do you see the Spirit at work in your church and community?

SESSION III

1. View Session III of the video presentation.
2. Compare and contrast a community centered in the Word with one centered in the Spirit.
3. How do you respond to the author's notion of a Spirit-filled piety?
4. What relation do you see between the Spirit and the church's polity?
5. What practices of your congregation seem to demonstrate the presence of the Spirit?

SESSION IV

1. View Session IV of the video presentation.
2. What evidence of the Spirit do you see outside the language and practices of the church?
3. In what ways does our situation compare with the first century? How can the early church be a model or source of influence for us today?
4. In light of the ideas you have dealt with in this text, what are the most compelling challenges facing your congregation?